In a WEEKEND
baby Afghans

Beach Baby, *page 8*

There is nothing more exciting than a new baby coming into one's life! The immediate thought for a crochet enthusiast is to make a special blanket to welcome the bundle of joy. But with the busyness of life, who has the time? You do!

Designer Karen McKenna has created 12 precious wraps that will make a quick completion a reality. Truly, these designs can be completed in a weekend (or less)! Ripples, in-the-round and allover stitch patterns are all included in this lovely collection. As a bonus, she's included multiple blanket sizes that will accommodate smaller needs such as a car seat or infant carrier. Whichever size you choose, you can create an extra special gift in just a few hours. Your thoughtfulness will be appreciated for years to come!

Table of Contents

2	Ahoy Matey
5	Country Boy
8	Beach Baby
11	Teddy Bear Blue
14	Sugar & Spice
17	Daddy's Girl
20	Wild Child
23	Raspberry Kisses
25	Angel
28	The Frog & the Peach
31	Light Breeze
34	Lemon Drop

General Information

38	Yarn Specifics
39	Stitch Guide
40	Metric Conversion Charts

Raspberry Kisses, *page 23*

Ahoy Matey

Skill Level

■■■□ INTERMEDIATE

Finished Sizes

Instructions given are for baby afghan; changes for car seat, small cradle and security blanket are given in [ ].

Finished Measurements

25 inches wide x 32 inches long *(baby afghan)* [20 inches wide x 24 inches long *(car seat)*, 13 inches wide x 29 inches long *(small cradle)*, 13 inches wide x 15 inches long *(security)*]

Materials

- Medium (worsted) weight acrylic/ cotton yarn:
    10½ oz/615 yds/300g white
    3½ oz/205 yds/100g each red and teal
  4 MEDIUM
- Size I/9/5.5mm crochet hook or size needed to obtain gauge
- Tapestry needle

See page 38 for Yarn Specifics.

Gauge

Chevron = 6½ inches; 12 rows = 4½ inches

Pattern Notes

Refer to Stitch Diagram as needed.

Weave in loose ends as work progresses.

Carry colors not in use up side.

Join with slip stitch as indicated unless otherwise stated.

Special Stitches

Long double crochet (lng dc): Yo, insert hook in indicated sc on 2nd row below, yo, pull up lp even with working row, [yo, pull through 2 lps] twice.

Extended long double crochet (ext lng dc): Yo, insert hook in indicated sc on 3rd row below, yo, pull up lp even with working row, [yo, pull through 2 lps] twice.

Afghan

Row 1 (RS): With white, ch 131 [98, 65, 65], sc in 2nd ch from hook, sc in each of next 14 chs, 3 sc in next ch, sc in each of next 15 chs, *sk next 2 chs, sc in each of 15 chs, 3 sc in next ch, sc in each of next 15 chs, rep from * across, turn. *(132 [99, 66, 66] sts)*

Row 2: Ch 1, sk first st, sc in each of next 15 sts, 3 sc in next st, *sc in each of next 15 sts, sk next 2 sts, sc in each of next 15 sts, 3 sc in next st, rep from * across to last 16 sts, sc in each of next 14 sts, sk next st, sc in last st, turn.

Rows 3 & 4: Rep row 2, **change color** *(see Stitch Guide and Pattern Notes)* to red in last st, turn. Drop white.

Row 5: With red, ch 1, sk first st, *sc in next st, **lng dc** *(see Special Stitches)* in next st on 2nd row below, [sc in next st, **ext lng dc** *(see Special Stitches)* in next st on 3rd row below, sc in next st, lng dc in next st on 2nd row below] 3 times, sc in next st, 3 sc in next st, sc in next st, lng dc in same st on 2nd row below as last lng dc worked, [sc in next st, ext lng dc in next st on 3rd row below, sc in next st, lng dc in next st on 2nd row below] 3 times**, sc in next st, sk next 2 sts, rep from * across, ending last rep at **, sk next st, sc in last st, turn.

Row 6: Rep row 2. At end of row, change color to white in last st, turn. Fasten off red.

Rows 7–10: Rep row 2. At end of last row, change color to teal, drop white.

Rows 11 & 12: Rep rows 5 and 6. At end of last row, change color to white in last st. Fasten off teal.

Rows 13–16: Rep row 2. At end of last row, change color to red in last st, drop white.

Rows 17–88 [17–64, 17–76, 17–40]: [Rep rows 5–16 consecutively] 6 [4, 5, 2] times. At end of last row, fasten off.

Side Edgings
Hold piece with RS facing and last row at top, **join** (*see Pattern Notes*) white in last st of last row, working across next side in ends of rows and over carried yarns, sc evenly sp across to last row, 2 sc in last row, sl st in first st on next side Fasten off.

Rep on opposite long side.

Finishing
Block lightly. ●

Ahoy Matey
Reduced Sample of Stitch Diagram
Note: Reps shown in gray.

6
4
2
1

STITCH KEY

⬭ Chain (ch)

+ Single crochet (sc)

Ⴧ Long double crochet (lng dc)

Ⴧ Extended long double crochet (ext lng dc)

Country Boy

Skill Level
 EASY

Finished Sizes
Instructions given are for baby afghan; changes for car seat, small cradle and security blanket are given in [ ].

Finished Measurements
24 inches wide x 30 inches long *(baby afghan)* [16 inches wide x 24 inches long *(car seat)*, 15 inches wide x 30 inches long *(small cradle)*, 13 inches wide x 16 inches long *(security)*]

Materials
- Light (DK) weight acrylic/wool/nylon yarn:
  3½ oz/288 yds/100g each off-white, beige and blue
- Size H/8/5mm crochet hook or size needed to obtain gauge
- Tapestry needle

See page 38 for Yarn Specifics.

Gauge
16 sts = 4 inches; 14 rows = 4 inches

Pattern Notes
Refer to Stitch Diagram as needed.

Weave in loose ends as work progresses.

Carry colors not in use up side.

Chain-3 at beginning of row counts as a double crochet unless otherwise stated.

Join with slip stitch as indicated unless otherwise stated.

Special Stitch
Single crochet join (sc join): Place slip knot on hook, insert hook in indicated st, yo and draw up a lp, yo and pull through both lps on hook.

Afghan
Foundation row: With off-white, ch 95 [65, 59, 53], dc in 4th ch from hook *(beg 3 sk chs count as a dc)*, dc in next ch, *ch 3, sk next 3 chs, dc in each of next 3 chs, rep from * across, **change color** *(see Stitch Guide and Pattern Notes)* to beige in last st, drop off-white, turn. *(48 [33, 30, 27] dc, 15 [10, 9, 8] ch-3 sps)*

Row 1: Ch 3 *(does not count as a st)*, sk first 3 dc, *working over next ch-3 sp, dc in each of 3 sk chs on foundation ch, ch 3, sk next 3 dc, rep from * across to beg ch-3, sc in 3rd ch of beg ch-3, change color to blue in last st, drop oats, turn. *(45 [30, 27, 24] dc, 16 [11, 10, 9] ch-3 sps, 1 sc)*

Row 2: Ch 3 *(see Pattern Notes)*, working over next ch-3 sp, dc in each of 2 sk dc on 2nd row below, *ch 3, sk next 3 dc, working over next ch-3 sp, dc in each of 3 sk dc on 2nd row below, rep from * across, change color to off-white in last st, drop blue, turn.

Row 3: Ch 3 *(does not count as a st)*, sk first 3 dc, *working over next ch-3 sp, dc in each of 3 sk dc on 2nd row below, ch 3, sk next 3 dc, rep from * across to last 3 sts, ch 3, sk next 2 dc, sc in 3rd ch of beg ch-3, change color to beige in last st, drop off-white, turn.

Rows 4–103 [4–83, 4–103, 4–55]: [Rep rows 2 and 3 alternately] 50 [40, 50, 26] times, working in established color sequence of 1 row of each color. At end of row 102 [82,102, 54], fasten off off-white. At end of row 103 [83, 103, 55], fasten off beige.

Row 104 [84, 104, 56]: With blue, ch 3, working over next ch-3 sp, dc in each of 2 sk dc on 2nd row below, hdc in each of next 3 dc, *working over next ch-3 sp, dc in each of 3 sk dc on 2nd row below, hdc in each of next 3 dc, rep from * across to last ch-3 sp, working over last ch-3 sp, dc in each of 3 sk dc on 2nd row below, turn.

Edging

Rnd 1: Now working in rnds, ch 1, 3 sc in same st as beg ch-1 *(corner)*, sc in each st across to last st, 3 sc in last st *(corner)*, working in ends of rows across next side and over carried yarns, work 106 sc evenly sp across, working in unused chs on opposite side of foundation ch, 3 sc in first ch *(corner)*, sc in each ch across to last ch, 3 sc in last ch *(corner)*, working in ends of rows across next side, work 106 sc evenly sp across to first sc, **join** *(see Pattern Notes)* in first sc, turn. Fasten off.

Rnd 2: Join beige with **sc join** *(see Special Stitch)* in 2nd sc of any corner, 2 sc in same sc as join, *sc in each sc across to 2nd sc of next corner, 3 sc in 2nd sc, rep from * twice, sc in each sc across to first sc, join in first sc, turn. Fasten off beige.

Rnd 3: Join off-white with sc in 2nd sc of any corner, 2 sc in same sc as join, *sc in each sc across to 2nd sc of next corner, 3 sc in 2nd sc, rep from * twice, sc in each sc across to first sc, join in first sc. Fasten off.

Finishing
Block lightly. ●

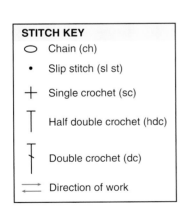

STITCH KEY

⬭	Chain (ch)
•	Slip stitch (sl st)
+	Single crochet (sc)
T	Half double crochet (hdc)
╀	Double crochet (dc)
⇄	Direction of work

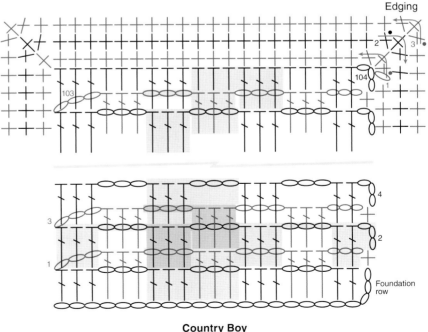

Country Boy
Reduced Sample of Stitch Diagram
Note: Reps shown in gray.

Beach Baby

Skill Level
 EASY

Finished Sizes
Instructions given are for baby afghan; changes for car seat, small cradle and security blanket are given in [ ].

Finished Measurements
24 inches wide x 30 inches long *(baby afghan)* [16 inches wide x 24 inches long *(car seat)*, 14 inches wide x 32 inches long *(small cradle)*, 14 inches wide x 16 inches long *(security)*]

Materials
- Medium (worsted) weight acrylic/ cotton yarn:
  7 oz/410 yds/200g each white, light blue and blue
- Size I/9/5.5mm crochet hook or size needed to obtain gauge
- Tapestry needle
- Stitch marker

See page 38 for Yarn Specifics.

Gauge
2 shell reps = 4 inches; 9 rows = 3½ inches

Pattern Notes
Refer to Stitch Diagram as needed.

Weave in loose ends as work progresses.

Chain-4 at beginning of row counts as a double crochet and chain-1 unless otherwise stated.

Carry colors not in use up side.

Color sequence is 4 rows each white, light blue and blue.

Join with slip stitch as indicated unless otherwise stated.

Chain-3 at beginning of round counts as a double crochet unless otherwise stated.

Special Stitches
Shell: 5 dc in indicated st.

V-stitch (V-st): (Dc, ch 1, dc) in indicated st.

Afghan
Row 1 (WS): With white, ch 92 [60, 52, 52], 2 dc in 4th ch from hook *(beg 3 sk chs count as a dc)*, sk next 2 chs, sc in each of next 3 chs, *sk next 2 chs, **shell** *(see Special Stitches)* in next ch, sk next 2 chs, sc in each of next 3 chs, rep from * across to last 3 chs, sk next 2 chs, 3 dc in last ch, turn. *(10 [6, 5, 5] shells, 6 dc, 33 [21, 18, 18] sc)*

Row 2 (RS): Ch 1, working in **back lps** *(see Stitch Guide)*, sc in each of first 2 sts, ch 1, sk next 2 sts, **V-st** *(see Special Stitches)* in next st, ch 1, *sk next 2 sts, sc in each of next 3 sts, ch 1, sk next 2 sts, V-st in next sc, ch 1, rep from * across to last 4 sts, sk next 2 sts, sc in each of last 2 sts, turn. *(11 [7, 6, 6] V-sts, 34 [22, 19, 19] sc, 22 [14, 12, 12] ch-1 sps)*

***Note:** Place marker to mark RS.*

Row 3: Ch 1, working through both lps, sc in each of first 2 sts, sk next ch-1 sp, shell in next ch-1 sp, *sk next ch-1 sp, sc in each of 3 sts, sk next ch-1 sp, shell in next ch-1 sp, rep from * across to last ch-1 sp, sk last ch-1 sp, sc in each of last 2 sts, turn. *(11 [7, 6, 6] shells, 34 [22, 19, 19] sc, 22 [14, 12, 12] ch-1 sps)*

Row 4: Ch 4 *(see Pattern Notes)*, working in back lps, dc in first sc, ch 1, sk next 2 sts, sc in each of next 3 sts, ch 1, *sk next 2 sts, V-st in next sc, ch 1, sk next 2 sts, sc in each of next 3 sts, ch 1, rep from * across to last 3 sts, sk next 2 sts, V-st in last st, **change color**

(see Stitch Guide and Pattern Notes) to light blue in last st, drop white. *(11 [7, 6, 6] V-sts, 2 dc, 33 [21, 18, 18] sc, 23 [15, 13, 13] ch-1 sps)*

Row 5: Ch 3, working through both lps, 2 dc in first dc, sk next 2 ch-1 sps, sc in each of next 3 sts, *sk next ch-1 sp, shell in next ch-1 sp, sk next ch-1 sp, sc in

each of next 3 sts, rep from * across to last 2 ch-1 sps, sk last 2 ch-1 sps, 3 dc in 3rd ch of beg ch-4, turn. *(10 [6, 5, 5] shells, 6 dc, 33 [21, 18, 18] sc)*

Row 6: Ch 1, working in back lps, sc in each of first 2 sts, ch 1, sk next 2 sts, V-st in next sc, ch 1, *sk next 2 sts, sc in each of next 3 sts, ch 1, sk next 2 sts, V-st in next st, ch 1, rep from * across to last 4 sts, sk next 2 sts, sc in each of last 2 sts, turn. *(11 [7, 6, 6] V-sts, 34 [22, 19, 19] sc)*

Row 7: Ch 1, working through both lps, sc in each of first 2 sts, sk next ch-1 sp, shell in next ch-1 sp, *sk next ch-1 sp, sc in each of next 3 sts, sk next ch-1 sp, shell in next ch-1 sp, rep from * across to last ch-1 sp, sk last ch-1 sp, sc in each of last 2 sts, turn. *(11 [7, 6, 6] shells, 34 [22, 19, 19] sc, 22 [14, 12, 12] ch-1 sps)*

Row 8: Ch 4, working in back lps, dc in first sc, ch 1, sk next 2 sts, sc in each of next 3 sts, ch 1, *sk next 2 sts, V-st in next st, ch 1, sk next 2 sts, sc in each of next 3 dc, ch 1, rep from * across to last 3 sts, sk next 2 sts, V-st in last st, change color to blue in last st, drop light blue, turn. *(11 [7, 6, 6] V-sts, 2 dc, 33 [21, 18, 18] sc, 23 [15, 13, 13] ch-1 sps)*

Rows 9–72 [9–56, 9–72, 9–40]): [Rep rows 5–8 consecutively] 16 [12, 16, 8] times, working in **color sequence** *(see Pattern Notes)*.

At end of last row, fasten off.

Edging

Rnd 1: With WS facing and last row at top, **join** *(see Pattern Notes)* white in first ch in upper right corner, ch 1, sc in same ch as beg ch-1, work 88 [55, 46, 47] sc evenly sp across to last st, 3 sc in last st, working across next side in ends of rows and over carried yarns, work 106 [91, 106, 72] sc evenly sp across, working across next side in unused lps on opposite side of foundation ch, 3 sc in first ch, work 89 [56, 47, 48] sc evenly sp across to last ch, 3 sc in last ch, working across next side in ends of rows and over carried yarns, work 106 [91, 106, 72] sc evenly sp across, 3 sc in first st of last row, join in first sc, turn. *(402 [306, 318, 252] sc)*

Rnd 2: Ch 3 *(see Pattern Notes)*, 4 dc in same sc as beg ch-3 *(beg shell)*, sk next 2 sc, sc in next sc, sk next 2 sc, *shell in next sc, sk next 2 sc, sc in next sc, sk next 2 sc, rep from * around, join in 3rd ch of beg ch-3. Fasten off. *(67 [51, 53, 42] shells)* ●

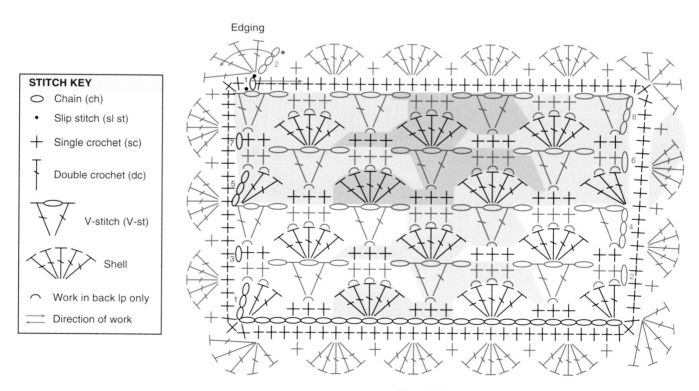

STITCH KEY
- ⬯ Chain (ch)
- • Slip stitch (sl st)
- + Single crochet (sc)
- ⊤ Double crochet (dc)
- V-stitch (V-st)
- Shell
- ⌢ Work in back lp only
- ⇄ Direction of work

Beach Baby
Reduced Sample of Stitch Diagram
Note: Reps shown in gray.

Teddy Bear Blue

Skill Level

 **EASY**

Finished Sizes

Instructions given are for baby afghan; changes for car seat, small cradle and security blanket are given in [ ].

Finished Measurements

26 inches wide x 31 inches long *(baby afghan)* [17 inches wide x 26 inches long *(car seat)*, 15 inches wide x 31 inches long *(small cradle)*, 14 inches wide x 17 inches long *(security)*]

Materials

- Medium (worsted) weight acrylic/wool yarn:
  3½ oz/200 yds/100g each off-white, light blue, medium blue and light brown
- Size J/10/6mm crochet hook or size needed to obtain gauge
- Tapestry needle
- Stitch marker

See page 38 for Yarn Specifics.

Gauge

4 blocks = 4½ inches; 4 rows = 2½ inches

Pattern Notes

Refer to Stitch Diagram as needed.

Weave in loose ends as work progresses.

Chain-3 at beginning of row counts as a double crochet unless otherwise stated.

Afghan

Row 1 (RS): With off-white, ch 84 [56, 52, 48], 2 dc in 4th ch from hook *(beg 3 sk chs count as a dc)*, *[sk next 3 chs, (sc, ch 3, 3 dc—*block made*) in next ch, rep from * across to last 4 chs, sk next 3 chs, sc in last ch, turn. *(19 [12, 11, 10] blocks, 3 dc, 1 sc)*

Note: *Place marker to mark RS.*

Row 2: Ch 3 *(see Pattern Notes)*, 2 dc in first st, sk next 3 sts, sc in next ch, ch 3, 3 dc in ch-3 sp, *sk next 4 sts, sc in next ch, ch 3, 3 dc in ch-3 sp, rep from * across to last 4 sts, sk next 3 sts, sc in 3rd ch of beg ch-3, turn. *(60 [39, 36, 33] dc, 1 sc, 19 [12, 11, 10] ch-3 sps)*

Row(s) 3–6 [3–5, 3–6, 3]: Rep row 2, **changing color** *(see Stitch Guide)* to light blue in last st at end of last row. Fasten off off-white.

Rows 7–12 [6–10, 7–12, 4–6]: Rep row 2, changing color to medium blue in last st at end of last row. Fasten off light blue.

Rows 13–18 [11–15, 13–18, 7–9]: Rep row 2, changing color to light brown in last st at end of last row. Fasten off medium blue.

Rows 19–30 [16–25, 19–30, 10–15]: Rep row 2, changing color to medium blue in last st at end of last row. Fasten off light brown.

Rows 31–36 [26–30, 31–36, 16–18]: Rep row 2, changing color to light blue at end of last row. Fasten off medium blue.

Rows 37–42 [31–35, 37–42, 19–21]: Rep row 2, changing color to off-white in last st at end of last row. Fasten off light blue.

Rows 43–48 [36–40, 43–48, 22–24]: Rep row 2, changing color to light brown in last st at end of row 48. Fasten off off-white.

Edging

Rnd 1: Now working in rnds, ch 1, 3 sc in first st *(corner)*, sc in each ch and in each sc across to last st, 3 sc in last st *(corner)*, working in ends of rows across next side, work 94 [78, 94, 46] sc evenly sp across, working across next side in unused lps on opposite side of foundation ch, 3 sc in first ch *(corner)*, sc in each ch across to last ch, 3 sc in last ch *(corner)*, working in ends of rows across next side, work 94 [78, 94, 46] sc evenly across, **join** *(see Pattern Notes)* in first sc, change color to medium blue by drawing lp through, turn. Fasten off light brown. *(343 [255, 279, 175] sc)*

Rnd 2: Ch 1, sc in same sc as beg ch-1, *sc in each sc across to 2nd sc of next corner, 3 sc in 2nd sc, rep from * 3 times, join in first sc, change color to light blue by drawing lp through, turn. Fasten off medium blue. *(351 [263, 287, 183] sc)*

Rnd 3: Ch 1, sc in same sc as beg ch-1 and in next sc, 3 sc in next sc, *sc in each sc across to 2nd sc of next corner, 3 sc in 2nd sc, rep from * twice, sc in each sc across to first sc, join in first sc, change color to off-white by drawing lp through, turn. Fasten off light blue. *(359 [271, 295, 191] sc)*

Rnd 4: Ch 1, sc in same st as beg ch-1, *sc in each sc across to 2nd sc of next corner, 3 sc in 2nd sc, rep from * 3 times, sc in each sc to first sc, join in first sc, Fasten off. *(367 [279, 303, 199] sc)*

Finishing
Block lightly. ●

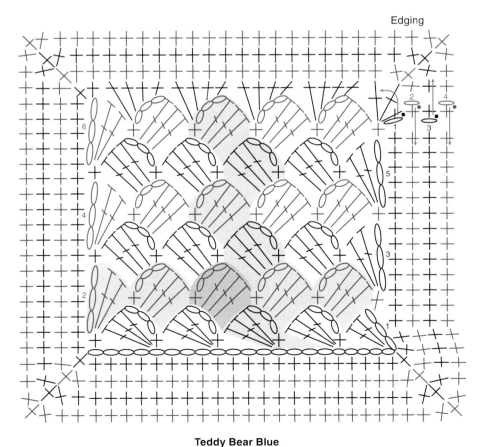

Edging

STITCH KEY

⬭	Chain (ch)
•	Slip stitch (sl st)
+	Single crochet (sc)
⊤	Double crochet (dc)
⟷	Direction of work

Teddy Bear Blue
Reduced Sample of Stitch Diagram
Note: Reps shown in gray.

Sugar & Spice

Skill Level
■■■□ INTERMEDIATE

Finished Sizes
Instructions given are for baby afghan; changes for car seat, small cradle and security blanket are given in [ ].

Finished Measurements
22 inches wide x 32 inches long *(baby afghan)* [17 inches wide x 25 inches long *(car seat)*, 17 inches wide x 32 inches long *(small cradle)*, 17 inches wide x 18 inches long *(security)*]

Materials
- Medium (worsted) weight nylon/ acrylic yarn:
  - 10½ oz/630 yds/300g white
  - 3½ oz/210 yds/100g each light pink, orange and light green
- Size J/10/6mm crochet hook or size needed to obtain gauge
- Tapestry needle

See page 38 for Yarn Specifics.

Gauge
Chevron (from point to point) = 6 inches; 7 rows = 4 inches

Pattern Notes
Refer to Stitch Diagram as needed.

Weave in loose ends as work progresses.

Join with slip stitch as indicated unless otherwise stated.

Special Stitch
V-stitch (V-st): (Dc, ch 1, dc) in indicated st.

Afghan
Row 1 (RS): With white, ch 107 [81, 81, 81], dc in 3rd ch from hook, *[sk next 2 chs, **V-st** *(see Special Stitch)* in next ch] 4 times, ch 3, V-st in next ch, [sk next 2 chs, V-st in next ch] 3 times, sk next 2 chs, **dc dec** *(see Stitch Guide)* in next 2 chs, rep from * across, **change color** *(see Stitch Guide)* to light pink in last st, turn. Fasten off-white. *(4 [3, 3, 3] chevrons)*

Row 2: Ch 1, **sc dec** *(see Stitch Guide)* in first 2 sts, ch 1, sk next ch-1 sp, [sc in each of next 2 sts, ch 1, sk next ch-1 sp] 3 times, sc in next st, (sc, ch 3, sc) in next ch-3 sp, sc in next st, ch 1, sk next ch-1 sp, [sc in each of next 2 sts, ch 1, sk next ch-1 sp] 3 times, *sk next st, sc in next st, ch 1, sk next st and next ch-1 sp, [sc in each of next 2 sts, ch 1, sk next ch-1 sp] 3 times, sc in next st, (sc, ch 3, sc) in next ch-3 sp, sc in next st, ch 1, sk next ch-1 sp, [sc in each of next 2 sts, ch 1, sk next ch-1 sp] 3 times, rep from * across to last 2 sts, sc dec in last 2 sts, change color to white in last st, turn. Fasten off light pink. *(69 [52, 52, 52] sc, 4 [3, 3, 3] ch-3 sps, 32 [24, 24, 24] ch-1 sps)*

Row 3: Ch 2, dc in next ch-1 sp, V-st in each of next 3 ch-1 sps, (V-st, ch 3, V-st) in next ch-3 sp, V-st in each of next 3 ch-1 sps, *dc dec in next 2 ch-1 sps, V-st in each of next 3 ch-1 sps, (V-st, ch 3, V-st) in next ch-3 sp, rep from * across to last ch-1 sp, dc dec in last ch-1 sp and last sc, change color to orange in last st, turn. Fasten off-white. *(32 [24, 24, 24] V-sts, 2 dc, 4 [3, 3, 3] ch-3 sps)*

Row 4: Rep row 2. At end of row, change color to white, fasten off orange.

Row 5: Rep row 3. At end of row, change color to light green, fasten off-white.

Row 6: Rep row 2. At end of row, change color to white, fasten off light green.

Row 7: Rep row 3. At end of row, change color to light pink fasten off-white.

Rows 8–55 [8–43, 8–55, 8–31]: [Rep rows 2–7 consecutively] 8 [6, 8, 4] times. At end of last row, do not change color. Fasten off.

Edging

Note: On rnd 1, ch-1 sps count as sts.

Rnd 1: With WS facing and last row at top, **join** *(see Pattern Notes)* white in first st in right-hand corner, ch 1, sc dec in same st as beg ch-1 and in next st, sc in each of next 11 sts, (sc, ch 3, sc) in next ch-3 sp, [sc in each of next 11 sts, sk next st, sc in next st, sk next st,

sc in each of next 11 sc, (sc, ch 3, sc) in next ch-3 sp] 3 [2, 2, 2] times, sc in each of next 11 sts, sc dec in next 2 sts, working in ends of rows across next side, 2 sc in side of last row, work 84 [64, 84, 46] sc evenly sp across to next corner, working in unused chs on opposite side of foundation ch, 2 sc in first ch, sc in each of next 11 chs, [sk next ch, sc in next ch, sk next ch, sc in each of next 11 chs, (sc, ch 3, sc) in next ch-1 sp, sc in each of 11 chs] 3 [2, 2, 2] times, sk next ch, sc in next ch, sk next ch, sc in each of next 11 chs, 2 sc in last ch, working in ends of rows across next side, work 83 [63, 83, 45] sc evenly sp across to last row, 2 sc in last row, join in first sc, turn. *(371 [281, 321, 245] sc)*

Rnd 2: Ch 1, sc in same sc as beg ch-1, sc in next sc, 2 sc in next sc, sc in each sc across to first sc of next corner, 2 sc in 2nd sc, [sc in each of next 11 sc, sk next sc, sc in next sc, sk next sc, sc in each of next 11 sc, (sc, ch 3, sc) in next ch-3 sp] twice [once, once, once], sc in each of next 11 sc, sk next sc, sc in next sc, sk next sc, sc in each of next 11 sc, 2 sc in next sc, sc in each sc across to next 2-sc corner, 2 sc in first sc of corner, sc in each of next 14 sc, [(sc, ch 3, sc) in next ch-3 sp, sc in each of next 11 sc, sk next sc, sc in next sc, sk next sc, sc in each of 11 sc] twice [once, once, once], (sc, ch 3, sc) in next ch-3 sp, sc in each of next 12 sc, join in first sc. Fasten off. *(378 [288, 328, 252] sc)*

Finishing
Block lightly. ●

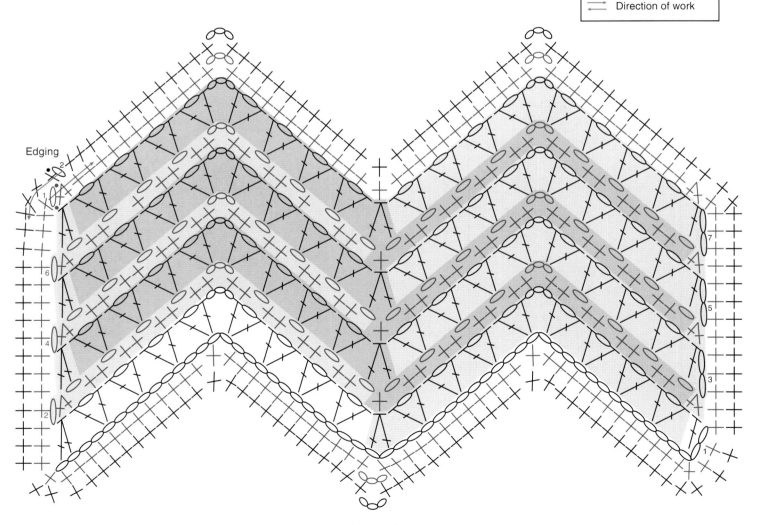

Edging

Sugar & Spice
Reduced Sample of Stitch Diagram
Note: Reps shown in gray.

Daddy's Girl

Skill Level

 EASY

Finished Sizes

Instructions given are for baby afghan; changes for car seat, small cradle and security blanket are given in [ ].

Finished Measurements

26 inches wide x 35 inches long *(baby afghan)* [17 inches wide x 24 inches long *(car seat)*, 15 inches wide x 30 inches long *(small cradle)*, 14 inches wide x 17 inches long *(security)*]

Materials

- Light (DK) weight acrylic yarn: 10½ oz/819 yds/300g pink 3½ oz/273 yds/100g each gray and dark gray
- Size H/8/5mm crochet hook or size needed to obtain gauge
- Tapestry needle

Note: See page 38 for Yarn Specifics.

Gauge

14 sts = 4 inches; 12½ rows = 4 inches

Pattern Notes

Refer to Stitch Diagram as needed.

Weave in loose ends as work progresses.

Chain-3 at beginning of row counts as a double crochet unless otherwise stated.

Join with slip stitch as indicated unless otherwise stated.

Afghan

Row 1 (RS): With pink, ch 82 [56, 50, 44], sc in 4th ch from hook *(beg 3 sk chs count as a dc)*, *dc in next ch, sc in next ch, rep from * across, turn. *(40 [27, 24, 21] dc, 40 [27, 24, 21] sc)*

Row 2: Ch 3 *(see Pattern Notes)*, *sc in next dc, dc in next sc, rep from * across to beg ch-3, sc in 3rd ch of beg ch-3, turn.

Row 3: Ch 3, *sc in next dc, dc in next sc, rep from * across to beg ch-3, sc in 3rd ch of beg ch-3, turn.

Rows 4–104 [4–72, 4–92, 4–50]: Rep row 3.

Edging

Rnd 1: Now working in rnds, ch 1, 3 sc in same st as beg ch-3 *(corner)*, *sc in each st across to last st, 3 sc in last st *(corner)*, working in ends of rows across next side, work 104 [72, 92, 50] sc evenly sp across, working across next side in unused lps on opposite side of foundation ch, 3 sc in first ch *(corner)*, work 78 [52, 46, 40] sc evenly sp across to last ch, 3 sc in last ch *(corner)*, working across next side in ends of rows, work 104 [72, 92, 50] sc evenly sp across to first sc, **join** *(see Pattern Notes)* in first sc, change color to dark gray by drawing lp through, turn. Fasten off pink. *(364 [248, 264, 192] sc)*

Rnd 2: Ch 1, sc in same sc as beg ch-1, *sc in each sc across to 2nd sc of next corner, 3 sc in 2nd sc, rep from * 3 times, join in first sc, change color to gray by drawing lp through, turn. Fasten off dark gray. *(372 [256, 272, 200] sc)*

Rnd 3: Ch 3, 2 dc same sc as beg ch-3, 3 dc in each rem sc around, join in 3rd ch of beg ch-3. Fasten off. *(1116 [768, 746, 600] dc)*

Finishing
Block lightly. ●

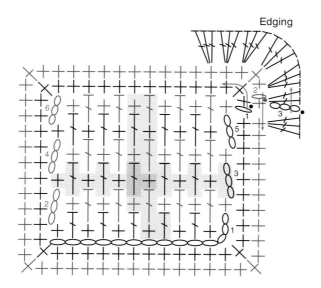

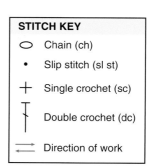

Daddy's Girl
Reduced Sample of Stitch Diagram
***Note:** Reps shown in gray.*

STITCH KEY	
⬭	Chain (ch)
•	Slip stitch (sl st)
+	Single crochet (sc)
┬	Double crochet (dc)
⇄	Direction of work

Wild Child

Skill Level

 EASY

Finished Sizes

Instructions given are for baby afghan; changes for car seat, small cradle and security blanket are given in [ ].

Finished Measurements

25 inches wide x 33 inches long *(baby afghan)* [17 inches wide x 23 inches long *(car seat)*, 15 inches wide x 28 inches long *(small cradle)*, 13 inches wide x 15 inches long *(security)*]

Materials

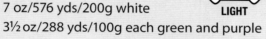

- Light (DK) weight acrylic/wool/nylon yarn:
  7 oz/576 yds/200g white
  3½ oz/288 yds/100g each green and purple
- Size H/8/5mm crochet hook or size needed to obtain gauge
- Tapestry needle

Note: *See page 38 for Yarn Specifics.*

Gauge

12 sts = 4 inches; 8 rows = 4¼ inches

Pattern Notes

Refer to Stitch Diagram as needed.

This blanket is made lengthwise. When cutting an end, leave at least 6-inch end to weave in.

Weave in loose ends as work progresses.

Chain-2 at beginning of row counts as first double crochet unless otherwise stated.

Chain-3 at beginning of row counts as first treble crochet unless otherwise stated.

Join with slip stitch as indicated unless otherwise stated.

Chain-2 at beginning of round counts as first half double crochet unless otherwise stated.

Special Stitch

Double treble decrease (dtr dec): Holding back last lp of each dtr, dtr in each of next 3 indicated sts, yo, draw through all lps on hook.

Afghan

Row 1 (WS): With green, ch 98 [66, 82, 42], hdc in 3rd ch from hook *(beg 2 sk chs count as a hdc)*, hdc in each rem ch across, **change color** *(see Stitch Guide)* to white in last st, turn. Fasten off holly. *(97 [65, 81, 41] hdc)*

Row 2 (RS): Ch 1, sc in first st, *hdc in next st , dc in next st, tr in next st, 3 **dtr** *(see Stitch Guide)* in next st, tr in next st, dc in next st, hdc in next st, sc in next st, rep from * across to last 8 sts, hdc in next st, dc in next st, tr in next st, 3 dtr in next st, tr in next st, dc in next st, hdc in next st, sc in 2nd ch of beg ch-2, change color to purple in last st, turn. Fasten off white. *(121 [81, 101, 51] sts)*

Row 3: Ch 2 *(see Pattern Notes)*, sk next st, dc in each of next 3 sts, *3 dc in st, dc in each of next 3 sts, **dc dec** *(see Stitch Guide)* in next 3 sts, dc in each of next 3 sts, rep from * across to last 6 sts, 3 dc in next st, dc in each of next 3 sts, sk next st, dc in last st, change color to white in last st, turn. Fasten off purple.

Row 4: Ch 3 *(see Pattern Notes)*, sk next st, tr in next st, dc in next st, hdc in next st, *sc in next st, hdc in next st, dc in next st, tr in next st, **dtr dec** *(see Special Stitch)* in next 3 sts, tr in next st, dc in next st, hdc in next st, rep from * across to last 6 sts, sc in next st, hdc in next st, dc in next st, tr in next st, sk next st,

tr in last, change to green in last st, turn. Fasten off-white. *(97 [65, 81, 41] sts)*

Row 5: Ch 2, hdc in each st across, change to white in last st, turn. Fasten off green.

Row 6: Ch 1, sc in first st, *hdc in next st, dc in next st, tr in next st, 3 dtr in next st , tr in next st, dc in next st, hdc in next st, sc in next st, rep from * across to last 8 sts, hdc in next st, dc in next st, tr in next st, 3 dtr in next st, tr in next st, dc in next st, hdc in next st, sc in last st, change color to purple in last st, turn. Fasten off-white. *(121 [81, 101, 51] sts)*

Rows 7–42 [7–30, 7–26, 7–22]: [Rep rows 3–6 consecutively] 9 [6, 5, 4] times.

Rows 43–45 [31–33, 27–29, 23–25]: Rep rows 3–5. At end of last row, do not change color.

Side Edgings

First Side
2 hdc in same st as last st of last row made, working in ends of rows across next side, hdc evenly sp across to row 1, 3 hdc in last row, **join** *(see Pattern Notes)* in first ch on opposite side of foundation ch. Fasten off.

2nd Side
Hold piece with same side facing and opposite short side at top, join green in side of row 1, ch 2, 2 hdc in same sp, working in ends of rows of side, hdc evenly sp across to first st of last row, 2 hdc in same st as

beg ch-2 of last row made, join in 2nd ch of beg ch-2. Fasten off.

Border

Rnd 1: Join white in 2nd hdc of any corner, **ch 2** *(see Pattern Notes)*, 2 hdc in same st as beg ch-2, *hdc evenly sp across side to 2nd hdc of next corner, 3 hdc in 2nd hdc, rep from * twice, hdc evenly sp across to beg ch-2, join in 2nd ch of beg ch-2, turn. Fasten off.

Rnd 2: Join purple in 2nd hdc of any corner, ch 2, 2 hdc in same st as beg ch-2, *hdc in each hdc across to 2nd hdc of next corner,

3 hdc in 2nd hdc, rep from * twice, hdc in each hdc across to beg ch-2, join in 2nd ch of beg ch-2, turn. Fasten off.

Finishing

Block lightly. ●

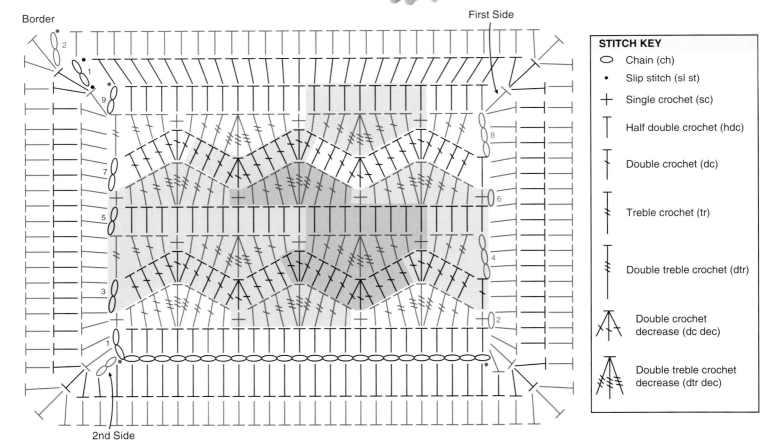

Border   First Side

STITCH KEY	
⬭	Chain (ch)
•	Slip stitch (sl st)
+	Single crochet (sc)
T	Half double crochet (hdc)
⊤	Double crochet (dc)
⊤	Treble crochet (tr)
⊤	Double treble crochet (dtr)
⋀	Double crochet decrease (dc dec)
⋀	Double treble crochet decrease (dtr dec)

2nd Side

Wild Child
Reduced Sample of Stitch Diagram
***Note:** Reps shown in gray.*

Raspberry Kisses

Skill Level

 EASY

Finished Sizes

Instructions given are for baby afghan; changes for car seat, small cradle and security blanket are given in [ ].

Finished Measurements

30 inches wide x 30 inches long *(baby afghan)* [20 inches wide x 20 inches long *(car seat)*, 20 inches wide x 20 inches long *(small cradle)*, 15 inches wide x 15 inches long *(security)*]

Materials

- Medium (worsted) weight acrylic yarn:
  17½ oz/900 yds/500g) raspberry

- Size L/11/8mm crochet hook or size needed to obtain gauge
- Tapestry needle

Note: *See page 38 for Yarn Specifics.*

Gauge

18½ sts = 8 inches; 8 rows = 4 inches

Pattern Notes

Refer to Stitch Diagram as needed.

Weave in loose ends as work progresses.

Edges may curl slightly while working.

Join with slip stitch as indicated unless otherwise stated.

Chain-6 at beginning of round counts as first double crochet and chain-3 unless otherwise stated.

Afghan

Rnd 1 (RS): Ch 5, **join** *(see Pattern Notes)* in first ch to form ring, **ch 6** *(see Pattern Notes)*, 4 dc in ring, [ch 3, 4 dc in ring] twice, ch 3, 3 dc in ring, join in 3rd ch of beg ch-6. *(16 dc, 4 ch-3 sps)*

Rnd 2: Sl st in next ch-3 sp, ch 6, dc in same sp as beg ch-6, *[**fpdc** *(see Stitch Guide)* around next dc, dc in next dc] twice, (dc, ch 3, dc) in next ch-3 sp, rep from * twice, [fpdc around next dc, dc in next dc] twice, join in 3rd ch of beg ch-6. *(24 sts)*

Rnd 3: Sl st in next ch-3 sp, ch 6, dc in same sp as beg ch-6, *[dc in next dc, fpdc around next fpdc] across to next ch-3 sp, (dc, ch 3, dc) in ch-3 sp, rep from * twice, [dc in next dc, fpdc around next fpdc] around to beg ch-6, join in 3rd ch of beg ch-6. *(32 sts)*

Rnd 4: Sl st in next ch-3 sp, ch 6, dc in same ch sp as beg ch-6, *[fpdc around next st, dc in next st] across to next ch-3 sp, (dc, ch 3, dc) in ch-3 sp, rep from * twice, [fpdc around next st, dc in next st] around to beg ch-6, join in 3rd ch of beg ch-6. *(40 sts)*

Rnds 5–30 [5–20, 5–20, 5–14]: [Rep rnds 3 and 4 alternately] 13 [8, 5, 8] times. *(248 [168, 120, 168] sts at end of last rnd)*

Edging

Rnd 1: Ch 1, sc in same st as beg ch-1, 5 sc in next ch-3 sp *(corner)*, *sc in each st across to next ch-3 sp, 5 sc in next ch-3 sp *(corner)*, rep from * twice, sc in each rem st around to first sc, join in first sc, turn.

Rnd 2: Ch 1, sc in same st as beg ch-1 and in each st across to 2nd sc of next corner, 3 sc in 2nd sc, *sc in each sc across to 2nd sc of next corner, 3 sc in 2nd sc, rep from * twice, sc in each sc to first sc, join in first sc.

Rnd 3: Ch 1, working left to right, **reverse sc** *(see Stitch Guide)* in each st around, join in first reverse sc. Fasten off.

Finishing
Block lightly. ●

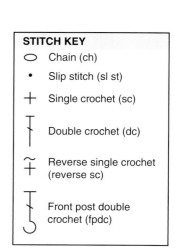
Edging

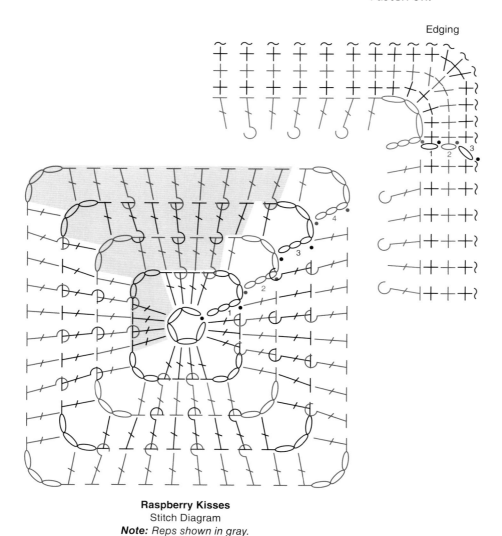

Raspberry Kisses
Stitch Diagram
***Note:** Reps shown in gray.*

STITCH KEY

⬭	Chain (ch)
•	Slip stitch (sl st)
+	Single crochet (sc)
⊤	Double crochet (dc)
≈	Reverse single crochet (reverse sc)
⌐	Front post double crochet (fpdc)

Angel

Skill Level
 EASY

Finished Sizes
Instructions given are for baby afghan; changes for car seat, small cradle and security blanket are given in [ ].

Finished Measurements
24 inches wide x 30 inches long *(baby afghan)* [17½ inches wide x 24 inches long *(car seat)*, 14 inches wide x 30 inches long *(small cradle)*, 14 inches wide x 17 inches long *(security)*]

Materials
- Light (DK) weight cotton yarn: 10½ oz/660 yds/300g white
- Size 7/4.5mm crochet hook or size needed to obtain gauge
- Tapestry needle

Note: *See page 38 for Yarn Specifics.*

Gauge
1 chevron (from point to point) = 3½ inches; 5 rows = 3 inches

Pattern Notes
Refer to Stitch Diagram as needed.

Weave in loose ends as work progresses.

Chain-3 at beginning of row counts as first double crochet and chain-1 unless otherwise stated.

Special Stitches
Double crochet decrease (dc dec): Holding back last lp of each dc on hook, dc in next ch or st, sk next 3 chs or sts, dc in next st, yo and draw through all 3 lps on hook.

Single crochet decrease (sc dec): Draw up lp in indicated st, sk next st, draw up lp in next st, yo and draw through all 3 lps on hook.

Afghan
Row 1 (RS): Ch 144 [104, 84, 84], dc in 4th ch from hook *(beg 3 sk chs count as first dc and ch-1)*, *[ch 1, sk next ch, dc in next ch] 3 times, ch 1, sk next ch, **dc dec** *(see Special Stitches)* in next 5 chs, [ch 1, sk next ch, dc in next ch] 3 times, ch 1, sk next ch**, (dc, ch 3, dc) in next ch, rep from * across, ending last rep at **, (dc, ch 1, dc) in last ch, turn. *(7 [5, 4, 4] chevrons)*

Row 2: Ch 3 (see Pattern Notes), dc in first st, [dc in next ch-1 sp, dc in next dc] 3 times, dc in next ch-1 sp, *dc dec in next 5 sts, [dc in next ch-1 sp, dc in next dc] 3 times**, (2 dc, ch 3, 2 dc) in next ch-3 sp, [dc in next dc, dc in next ch-1 sp] 3 times, rep from * across, ending last rep at **, (dc, ch 1, dc) in 2nd ch of beg ch-3, turn. *(118 [84, 67, 67] dc, 6 [4, 3, 3] ch-3 sps, 1 ch-1 sp)*

Row 3: Ch 3, dc in first dc, ch 1, sk next ch, *[dc in next dc, ch 1, sk next dc] 3 times, dc dec in next 5 sts, [ch 1, sk next dc, dc in next st] 3 times, ch 1**, (dc, ch 3, dc) in next ch-3 sp, ch 1, rep from * across, ending last rep at **, (dc, ch 1, dc) in 2nd ch of beg ch-3, turn. *(63 [44, 36, 36] dc, 6 [4, 3, 3] ch-3 sps, 57 [41, 33, 33] ch-1 sps)*

Row 4: Ch 3, dc in first st, [dc in next ch-1 sp, dc in next dc] 3 times, dc in next ch-1 sp, *dc dec in next 5 sts, [dc in next ch-1 sp, dc in next dc] 3 times**, (2 dc, ch 3, 2 dc) in next ch-3 sp, [dc in next dc, dc in next ch-1 sp] 3 times, rep from * across, ending last rep at **, (dc, ch 1, dc) in 2nd ch of beg ch-3, turn. *(118 [84, 67, 67] dc, 6 [4, 3, 3] ch-3 sps, 1 ch-1 sp)*

Rows 5–50 [5–40, 5–50, 5–28]: [Rep rows 3 and 4 alternately] 23 [18, 23, 12] times.

Edging

Ch 1, working across next side in ends of rows, work 100 [80, 100, 56] sc evenly sp across, working across next side in unused lps on opposite side of foundation ch, 2 sc in first ch, sc in each of next 9 chs, 3 sc in next ch, *sc in each of next 8 sts, **sc dec** (see Special Stitches) in next 3 chs, sc in each of next 8 chs, 3 sc in next ch, rep from * 5 [3, 2, 2] times, sc in each of next 9 chs, 2 sc in last ch, working across next side, work 100 [80, 100, 56] sc evenly sp across to beg ch-3 of last row, working across next side, 2 sc in 2nd ch of beg ch-2, sc in next ch, sc in each of next 7 sts, sc dec in next 3 sts, **sc in each of next 7 sts, sc in next ch of next ch-3 sp, 3 sc in next ch, sc in next ch, sc in each of next 7 sts, sc dec in next 3 sts, rep from ** 5 [3, 2, 2] times, sc in each of next 7 sts, sc in next ch, 2 sc in last st, join with sl st in first sc. Fasten off. *(486 [366, 321, 238] sc)*

Finishing
Block lightly. ●

STITCH KEY	
⬯	Chain (ch)
•	Slip stitch (sl st)
+	Single crochet (sc)
╎	Double crochet (dc)
⋀	Double crochet decrease (dc dec)
⋈	Single crochet decrease (sc dec)

Edgin

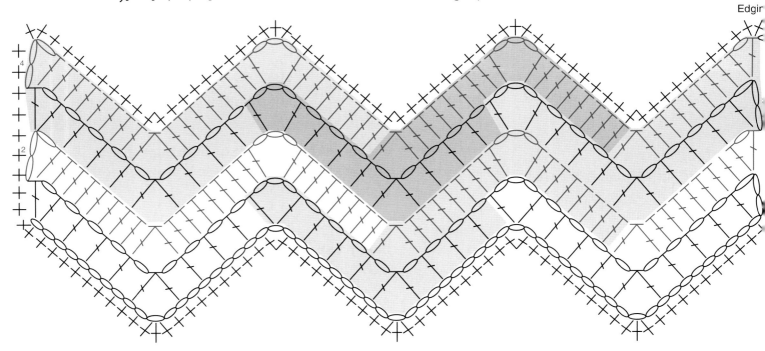

Angel
Reduced Sample of Stitch Diagram
Note: Reps shown in gray.

The Frog & the Peach

Skill Level

 **EASY**

Finished Sizes

Instructions given are for baby afghan; changes for car seat, small cradle and security blanket are given in [ ].

Finished Measurements

24 inches wide x 30 inches long *(baby afghan)* [16 inches wide x 24 inches long *(car seat)*, 15 inches wide x 30 inches long *(small cradle)*, 13 inches wide x 16 inches long *(security)*]

Materials

- Medium (worsted) weight acrylic yarn:
  7 oz/360 yds/200g each
  lime and coral
- Size I/9/5.5mm crochet hook or size needed to obtain gauge
- Tapestry needle

4

MEDIUM

Note: See page 38 for Yarn Specifics.

Gauge

4 blocks = 4½ inches; 8 rows = 5 inches

Pattern Notes

Refer to Stitch Diagram as needed.

Weave in loose ends as work progresses.

Carry color not in use up side.

Chain-4 at beginning of row counts as first treble crochet unless otherwise stated.

Chain-2 at beginning of round counts as first half double crochet unless otherwise stated.

Join with slip stitch as indicated unless otherwise stated.

Afghan

Row 1: With lime, ch 88 [80, 72, 68], sc in 2nd ch from hook, hdc in next ch, dc in next ch, sk next 3 chs, sc in next ch, ch 4, *sc in 2nd ch from hook, hdc in next ch, dc in next ch, sk next 3 chs, sc in next ch, ch 4, rep from * across, **change color** *(see Stitch Guide and Pattern Notes)* to coral in last st, drop lime, turn. *(21 [19, 17, 16] blocks)*

Row 2: Ch 4 *(see Pattern Notes)*, dc in next st, hdc in next st, sc in next st, *tr in next sc, dc in next st, hdc in next st, sc in next st, rep from * across, turn.

Row 3: *Ch 4 *(does not count as a st)*, sc in 2nd ch from hook, hdc in next ch, dc in next ch, sk next 3 sts, sc in next tr, rep from * across, ending with sc in 4th ch of beg ch-4, change color to lime in last st, drop coral, turn. *(84 (76, 68, 64] sts)*

Rows 4–47 [4–35, 4–47, 4–23]: [Rep rows 2 and 3 alternately] 22 [16, 21, 10] times, changing colors every 2 rows.

Row 48 [36, 48, 24]: Rep row 2. At end of row, do not turn.

Edging

Rnd 1: With lime, **ch 2** *(see Pattern Notes)*, working across side in ends of rows and over carried yarns, work 92 [68, 88, 44] hdc evenly sp across, working across next side in unused lps of foundation ch, 3 hdc in first ch, hdc in each ch across to last ch, 3 hdc in last ch, working across next side, work 92 [68, 88, 44] hdc evenly sp across, working across next side, 3 hdc in 4th ch of beg ch-4, hdc in each st across to beg ch-2, 2 hdc in same st as beg ch-2,

join *(see Pattern Notes)* in 2nd ch of beg ch-2, change color to coral by drawing lp through, turn. Fasten off lime. *(366 [302, 326, 230] hdc)*

Rnd 2: Ch 2, 3 hdc in next hdc, *hdc in each hdc across to 2nd hdc of next corner, 3 hdc in 2nd hdc, rep from * twice, hdc in each hdc to 2nd ch of beg ch-2, join in 2nd ch of beg ch-2. Fasten off. *(372 [310, 334, 238] hdc)*

Finishing
Block lightly. ●

STITCH KEY	
⬭	Chain (ch)
•	Slip stitch (sl st)
+	Single crochet (sc)
T	Half double crochet (hdc)
⊤	Double crochet (dc)
⊤	Treble crochet (tr)

Edging

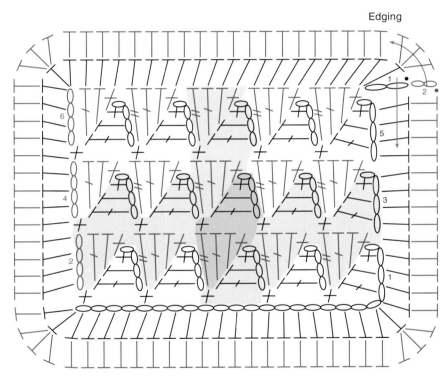

The Frog & the Peach
Reduced Sample of Stitch Diagram
Note: Reps shown in gray.

Light Breeze

Skill Level
 EASY

Finished Sizes
Instructions given are for baby afghan; changes for car seat, small cradle and security blanket are given in [ ].

Finished Measurements
30½ inches wide x 30½ inches long *(baby afghan)* [20½ inches wide x 20½ inches long *(car seat)*, 22½ inches wide x 32½ inches long *(small cradle)*, 15½ inches wide x 15½ inches long *(security)*]

Materials
- Medium (worsted) weight nylon/acrylic yarn:
  10½ oz/720 yds/300g multicolored
- Size I/9/5.5mm crochet hook or size needed to obtain gauge
- Tapestry needle
- **Note:** *See page 38 for Yarn Specifics.*

Gauge
Rnds 1–3 = 5½ inches

Pattern Notes
Refer to Stitch Diagram as needed.

Weave in loose ends as work progresses.

Join with slip stitch as indicated unless otherwise stated.

Chain-3 at beginning of round counts as first double crochet unless otherwise stated.

Chain-2 at beginning of round counts as first half double crochet unless otherwise stated.

Special Stitches
Beginning corner (beg corner): Ch 3, (2 dc, ch 3, 3 dc) in indicated sp.

Corner: (3 dc, ch 3, 3 dc) in indicated sp.

Afghan
Rnd 1: Ch 4, **join** *(see Pattern Notes)* in first ch to form ring, **ch 3** *(see Pattern Notes)*, 2 dc in ring, ch 3, [3 dc in ring, ch 3] 3 times, join in 3rd ch of beg ch-3. *(12 dc, 4 ch-3 sps)*

Rnd 2: Sl st in each of next 2 dc and in next ch-3 sp, **beg corner** *(see Special Stitches)* in same sp, ch 2, [**corner** *(see Special Stitches)* in next ch-3 sp, ch 2] 3 times, join in 3rd ch of beg ch-3. *(24 dc, 4 ch-3 sps, 4 ch-2 sps)*

Rnd 3: Sl st in each of next 2 dc and in next ch-3 sp, beg corner in same sp, *ch 2, 3 dc in next ch-2 sp, ch 2, corner in ch-3 sp of next corner, rep from * twice, ch 2, 3 dc in next ch-2 sp, ch 2, join in 3rd ch of beg ch-3. *(36 dc, 4 ch-3 sps, 8 ch-2 sps)*

Rnd 4: Sl st in each of next 2 dc and in next ch-3 sp, beg corner in same sp, *[ch 2, 3 dc in next ch-2 sp] twice, ch 2, corner in ch-3 sp of next corner, rep from * twice, [ch 2, 3 dc in ch-2 sp] twice, ch 2, join in 3rd ch of beg ch-3. *(48 dc, 4 ch-3 sps, 12 ch-2 sps)*

Rnd 5: Sl st in each of next 2 dc and in next ch-3 sp, beg corner in same sp, *[ch 2, 3 dc in ch-2 sp] 3 times, ch 2, corner in ch-3 sp of next corner, rep from * twice, [ch 2, 3 dc in next ch-2 sp] 3 times, ch 2, join in 3rd ch of beg ch-3. *(60 dc, 4 ch-3 sps, 16 ch-2 sps)*

Rnd 6: Sl st in each of next 2 dc and in next ch-3 sp, beg corner in same sp, *[ch 2, 3 dc in next ch-2 sp] across to next corner, ch 2, corner in ch-3 sp of next corner, rep from * twice, [ch 2, 3 dc in next ch-2 sp] across to beg ch-3, ch 2, join in 3rd ch of beg ch-3. *(72 dc, 4 ch-3 sps, 20 ch-2 sps)*

Rnds 7–11: Rep rnd 6. *(132 dc, 4 ch-3 sps, 40 ch-2 sps at end of last rnd)*

Size Small Cradle Only
Continue with Edging.

Sizes Baby Afghan, Car Seat & Security Only
Rnds 12–15: Rep rnd 6. *(180 dc, 4 ch-3 sps, 56 ch-2 sps at end of last rnd)*

Size Security Only
Continue with Edging.

Sizes Baby Afghan & Car Seat Only
Rnds 16 & 17: Rep rnd 6. *(204 dc, 4 ch-3 sps, 64 ch-2 sps at end of last rnd)*

Size Car Seat Only
Continue with Edging.

Size Baby Afghan Only
Rnds 18–25: Rep rnd 6. *(300 dc, 4 ch-3 sps, 96 ch-2 sps at end of last rnd)*

Edging
Rnd 1: Ch 2 *(see Pattern Notes)*, hdc in each of next 2 sts, 3 hdc in next ch-3 sp, *hdc in each st and ch across to next corner ch-3 sp, 3 hdc in 2nd ch of ch-3 sp, rep from * twice, hdc in each st across to beg ch-2, join in 2nd ch of beg ch-2, turn. *(504 [344, 304, 224] hdc)*

Rnd 2: Ch 2, *hdc in each st across to 2nd hdc of next corner, 3 hdc in 2nd hdc, rep from * 3 times, hdc in each st to beg ch-2, join in 2nd ch of beg ch-2, turn. Fasten off. *(512 [352, 312, 232] hdc)*

Finishing
Block lightly. ●

STITCH KEY

⬭	Chain (ch)
•	Slip stitch (sl st)
⊤	Half double crochet (hdc)
⊤	Double crochet (dc)

Edging

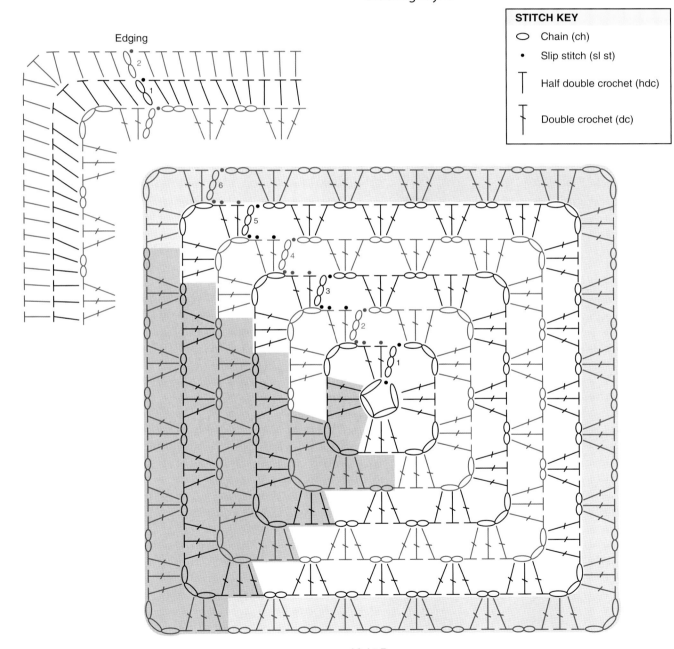

Light Breeze
Stitch Diagram
***Note:** Reps shown in gray.*

Lemon Drop

Skill Level
■■■■▷ EXPERIENCED

Finished Sizes
Instructions given for are baby afghan; changes for car seat, small cradle and security blanket are given in [ ].

Finished Measurements
32 inches point to point *(baby afghan)* [21 inches point to point *(car seat)*, 23 inches point to point *(small cradle)*, 15½ inches point to point *(security)*]

Materials
- Medium (worsted) weight acrylic yarn:
  17½ oz/1,125 yds/500g yellow
- Size I/9/5.5mm crochet hook or size needed to obtain gauge
- Tapestry needle

Note: *See page 38 for Yarn Specifics.*

Gauge
17 sts = 4½ inches, 8½ rows = 4 inches

Pattern Notes
Refer to Stitch Diagram as needed.

Weave in loose ends as work progresses.

Join with slip stitch as indicated unless otherwise stated.

Chain-3 at beginning of round counts as first double crochet unless otherwise stated.

Chain-4 at beginning of round counts as first double crochet and chain-1 unless otherwise stated.

Afghan
Rnd 1: Ch 4, **join** *(see Pattern Notes)* in first ch to form ring, **ch 3** *(see Pattern Notes)*, dc in ring, ch 1, [2 dc in ring, ch 1] 5 times, join in 3rd ch of beg ch-3. *(12 dc, 6 ch-1 sps)*

Rnd 2: Sl st in next dc and in next ch-1 sp, **ch 4** *(see Pattern Notes)*, dc in same sp as beg ch-4, *fpdc *(see Stitch Guide)* around each of next 2 sts, (dc, ch 1, dc) in next ch-1 sp, rep from * 4 times, fpdc around each of next 2 sts, join in 3rd ch of beg ch-4. *(24 sts, 6 ch-1 sps)*

Rnd 3: Sl st in next ch-1 sp, ch 4, dc in same sp as beg ch-4, *fpdc around each of next 4 sts, (dc, ch 1, dc) in next ch-1 sp, rep from * 4 times, fpdc around each of next 4 sts, join in 3rd ch of beg ch-4. *(36 sts, 6 ch-1 sps)*

Rnd 4: Sl st in next ch-1 sp, ch 4, dc in same sp as beg ch-4, *dc in next dc, sk next 2 fpdc, **fptr** *(see Stitch Guide)* around each of next 2 fpdc, working in front of fptr just made, fptr around each of next 2 sk fpdc, dc in next dc**, (dc, ch 1, dc) in next ch-1 sp, rep from * 5 times, ending last rep at **, join in 3rd ch of beg ch-4. *(48 sts, 6 ch-1 sps)*

Rnd 5: Sl st in next ch-1 sp, ch 4, dc in same sp as beg ch-4, *dc in each of next 2 dc, fpdc around each of next 4 fptr, dc in each of next 2 dc**, (dc, ch 1, dc) in ch-1 sp, rep from * 5 times, ending last rep at **, join in 3rd ch of beg ch-4. *(60 sts, 6 ch-1 sps)*

Rnd 6: Sl st in next ch-1 sp, ch 4, dc in same sp as beg ch-4, *fpdc next dc, dc in each of next 2 sts, sk next 2 fpdc, fptr around each of next 2 fpdc, working in front of fptr just made, fptr around each of next 2 sk fpdc, dc in each of next 2 dc, fpdc around next dc**, (dc, ch 1, dc) in next ch-1 sp, rep from * 5 times, ending last rep at **, join in 3rd ch of beg ch-4. *(72 sts, 6 ch-1 sps)*

Rnd 7: Sl st in next ch-1 sp, dc in same sp as beg ch-4, *fpdc around each of next 2 sts, dc in each of next 2 dc, fpdc around each of next 4 fptr, dc in each of next 2 dc, fpdc around each of next 2 sts**, (dc, ch 1, dc) in next ch-1 sp, rep from * 5 times, ending last rep at **, join in 3rd ch of beg ch-4. *(84 sts, 6 ch-1 sps)*

Rnd 8: Sl st in ch-1 sp, ch 4, dc in same sp as beg ch-4, *fpdc around each of next 3 sts, dc in each of next 2 dc, sk next 2 fpdc, fptr around each of next 2 fpdc, working in front of fptr just made, fptr around each of next 2 sk fpdc, dc in each of next 2 dc, fpdc around each of next 3 sts**, (dc, ch 1, dc) in next ch-1 sp, rep from * 5 times, ending last rep at **, join in 3rd ch of beg ch-4. *(96 sts, 6 ch-1 sps)*

Rnd 9: Sl st in next ch-1 sp, ch 4, dc in same sp as beg ch-4, *[fpdc around each of next 4 sts, dc in each of next 2 dc] twice, fpdc around each of next 4 sts**, (dc, ch 1, dc) in next ch-1 sp, rep from * 5 times, ending last rep at **, join in 3rd ch of beg ch-4. *(108 sts, 6 ch-1 sps)*

Rnd 10: Sl st in next ch-1 sp, ch 4, dc in same sp as beg ch-4, *dc in next dc, [sk next 2 fpdc, fptr around each of next 2 fpdc, working in front of fptr just made, fptr around each of next 2 sk fpdc, dc in each of next 2 dc] to last 5 sts before next ch-1 sp, sk next 2 fpdc, fptr around each of next 2 fpdc, working in front of fptr just made, fptr around each of first and 2nd sk fpdc, dc in next dc**, (dc, ch 1, dc) in next ch-1 sp, rep from * 5 times, ending last rep at **, join in 3rd ch of beg ch-4. *(120 sts, 6 ch-1 sps)*

Rnd 11: Sl st in next ch-1 sp, ch 4, dc in same sp as beg ch-4, *dc in each of next 2 dc, [fpdc around each of next 4 fptr, dc in each of next 2 dc] across to next ch-1 sp**, (dc, ch 1, dc) in next ch-1 sp, rep from * 5 times, ending last rep at **, join in 3rd ch of beg ch-4. *(132 sts, 6 ch-1 sps)*

Rnd 12: Sl st in next ch-1 sp, ch 4, dc in same sp as beg ch-4, *fpdc around next dc, dc in each of next 2 dc, [sk next 2 fpdc, fptr around each of next 2 fpdc, working in front of fptr just made, fptr around each of next 2 sk fpdc, dc in each of next 2 dc] across to last st before next ch-1 sp, fpdc around next dc**, (dc, ch 1, dc) in next ch-1 sp, rep from * 5 times, ending last rep at **, join in 3rd ch of beg ch-4. *(1440 sts, 6 ch-1 sps)*

Rnd 13: Sl st in next ch-1 sp, ch 4, dc in same sp as beg ch-4, *fpdc around each of next 2 sts, dc in each of next 2 dc, [fpdc around each of next 4 fptr, dc in each of next 2 dc] across to last 2 sts before next ch-1 sp, fpdc around each of next 2 sts**, (dc, ch 1, dc) in next ch-1 sp, rep from * 5 times, ending last rep at **, join in 3rd ch of beg ch-4. *(156 sts, 6 ch-1 sps)*

Rnd 14: Sl st in next ch-1 sp, ch 4, dc in same sp as beg ch-4, *fpdc around each of next 3 sts, [dc in each of next 2 dc, sk next 2 fpdc, fptr around each of next 2 fpdc, working in front of fptr just made, fptr around each of 2 sk fpdc] across to last 5 sts before next ch-1 sp, dc in each of next 2 dc, fpdc around each of next 3 sts**, (dc, ch 1, dc) in next ch-1 sp, rep from * 5 times, ending last rep at **, join in 3rd ch of beg ch-4. *(168 sts, 6 ch-1 sps)*

Rnd 15: Sl st in next ch-1 sp, ch 4, dc in same sp as beg ch-4, *fpdc around each of next 4 sts, [dc in each of next 2 dc, fpdc around each of next 4 fptr] across to last 6 sts before next ch-1 sp, dc in each of next 2 dc, fpdc around each of next 4 sts**, (dc, ch 1, dc) in next ch-1 sp, rep from * 5 times, ending last rep at **, join in 3rd ch of beg ch-4. *(180 sts, 6 ch-1 sps)*

Size Security Blanket Only
Continue with Edging.

Sizes Baby Afghan, Small Cradle & Car Seat Only
Rnds 16–21: Rep rnds 10–15. *(252 sts, 6 ch-1 sps at end of last rnd)*

Small Cradle Only
Continue with Edging.

Sizes Baby Afghan & Car Seat Only
Rnds 22 & 23: Rep rnds 10 and 11. *(276 sts, 6 ch-1 sps at end of last rnd)*

Size Car Seat Only
Continue with Edging.

Size Baby Afghan Only
Rnds 24–27: Rep rnds 12–15. *(304 sts, 6 ch-1 sps at end of last rnd)*

Rnds 28–32: Rep rnds 10–15. *(364 sts, 6 ch-1 sps at end of last rnd)*

Rnd 33: Sl st in next ch-1 sp, ch 4, dc in same sp as beg ch-4, *fpdc around next dc, fpdc around each of next 3 fpdc, dc in each of next 2 dc, [fpdc around each of next 4 fptr, dc in each of next 2 dc] 9 times, fpdc around each of next 4 sts**, (dc, ch 1, dc) in ch-1 sp, rep from * 5 times, ending last rep at **, join in 3rd ch of beg ch-4. *(376 sts, 6 ch-1 sps)*

Edging
Sl st in next ch-1 sp, (sc, ch 1, sc) in same ch-1 sp as beg ch-1, [sc in each st to next ch-1 sp, (sc, ch 1, sc) in next ch-1 sp] 5 times, sc in each st to first sc, join in first sc. Fasten off. *(388 [288, 264, 192] sc, 6 ch-1 sps)*

Finishing
Block lightly. ●

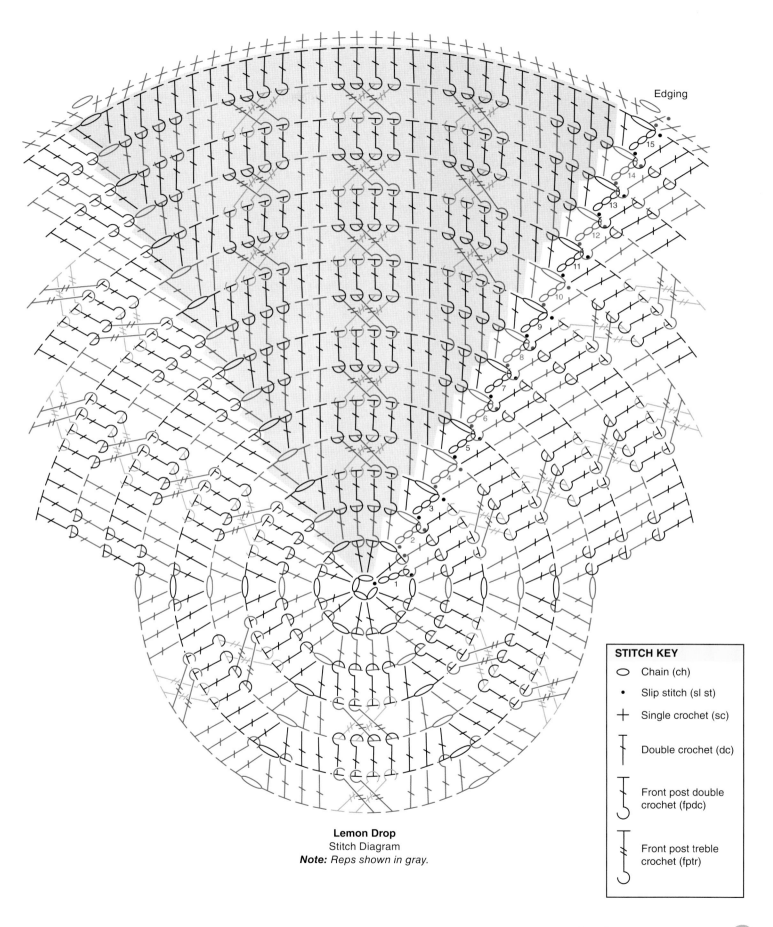

Edging

15
14
13
12
11
10
9
8
7
6
5
4
3
2
1

Lemon Drop
Stitch Diagram
Note: Reps shown in gray.

STITCH KEY

⬭   Chain (ch)

•   Slip stitch (sl st)

+   Single crochet (sc)

†   Double crochet (dc)

    Front post double
    crochet (fpdc)

    Front post treble
    crochet (fptr)

YARN SPECIFICS

The projects in this book were made with a variety of yarns in medium (worsted) and light (DK) weight. Please refer to the specific project instructions for the yarn weight used, recommended gauge and the number of yards required. Below we have listed the yarns used for our photography models as well as appropriate substitutes.

Ahoy Matey

- Berroco Weekend medium (worsted) weight acrylic/cotton yarn (3½ oz/205 yds/100g per hank):
    3 hanks #5900 daisy
    1 hank each #5955 reddy and #5942 cerulean

Country Boy

- Berroco Vintage DK light (DK) weight acrylic/wool/nylon yarn (3½ oz/288 yds/100g per hank):
    1 hank each #2101 mochi, #2105 oats and #2187 dungaree

Beach Baby

- Berroco Weekend medium (worsted) weight acrylic/cotton yarn (3½ oz/205 yds/100g per hank):
    2 hanks each #5902 vanilla, #5914 icy blue and #5982 coast

Teddy Bear Blue

- Plymouth Yarn Encore medium (worsted) weight acrylic/wool yarn (3½ oz/200 yds/100g per skein):
    1 skein each #0256 ecru, #0793 light blue, #0515 wedgewood and #6002 Rimouski

Sugar & Spice

- Berroco Comfort medium (worsted) weight nylon/acrylic yarn (3½ oz/210 yds/100g per skein):
    3 skeins #9700 chalk
    1 skein each #9704 peach, #9783 persimmon and #9740 seedling

Daddy's Girl

- Universal Yarn Uptown DK light (DK) weight acrylic yarn (3½ oz/273 yds/100g per skein):
    3 skeins #143 baby pink
    1 skein each #131 granite and #130 donahue

Wild Child

- Berroco Vintage DK light (DK) weight acrylic/wool/nylon yarn (3½ oz/288 yds/100g per hank):
    2 hanks #2100 snow day
    1 hank each #2135 holly and #2155 delphinium

Raspberry Kisses

- Universal Yarn Uptown Worsted medium (worsted) weight acrylic yarn (3½ oz/180 yds/100g per ball):
    5 balls #332 plum

Angel

- Cascade Yarns Ultra Pima light (DK) weight cotton yarn (3½ oz/220 yds/100g per skein):
    3 skeins #3728 white

The Frog & the Peach

- Universal Yarn Uptown Worsted medium (worsted) weight acrylic yarn (3½ oz/180 yds/100g per ball):
    2 balls each #314 lime and #344 coral

Light Breeze

- Cascade Yarns Cherub Aran medium (worsted) weight nylon/acrylic yarn (3½ oz/240 yds/100g per skein):
    3 skeins #505 rainbow brights

Lemon Drop

- Cascade Yarns Sateen Worsted medium (worsted) weight acrylic yarn (3½ oz/225 yds/100g per skein):
    5 skeins #20 lemonade

YARN SUBSTITUTES

Light (DK) Weight:

- Caron Simply Soft Light
- Plymouth Yarn Dreambaby Dk
- Universal Yarn Bamboo Pop

Medium (Worsted) Weight:

- Caron Simply Soft
- Premier Yarns Deborah Norville Everyday Soft Worsted
- Red Heart Super Saver

STITCH GUIDE

STITCH ABBREVIATIONS

beg	begin/begins/beginning
bpdc	back post double crochet
bpsc	back post single crochet
bptr	back post treble crochet
CC	contrasting color
ch(s)	chain(s)
ch-	refers to chain or space previously made (i.e., ch-1 space)
ch sp(s)	chain space(s)
cl(s)	cluster(s)
cm	centimeter(s)
dc	double crochet (singular/plural)
dc dec	double crochet 2 or more stitches together, as indicated
dec	decrease/decreases/decreasing
dtr	double treble crochet
ext	extended
fpdc	front post double crochet
fpsc	front post single crochet
fptr	front post treble crochet
g	gram(s)
hdc	half double crochet
hdc dec	half double crochet 2 or more stitches together, as indicated
inc	increase/increases/increasing
lp(s)	loop(s)
MC	main color
mm	millimeter(s)
oz	ounce(s)
pc	popcorn(s)
rem	remain/remains/remaining
rep(s)	repeat(s)
rnd(s)	round(s)
RS	right side
sc	single crochet (singular/plural)
sc dec	single crochet 2 or more stitches together, as indicated
sk	skip/skipped/skipping
sl st(s)	slip stitch(es)
sp(s)	space(s)/spaced
st(s)	stitch(es)
tog	together
tr	treble crochet
trtr	triple treble
WS	wrong side
yd(s)	yard(s)
yo	yarn over

YARN CONVERSION

OUNCES TO GRAMS	GRAMS TO OUNCES
1................28.4	25.................⅞
2................56.7	40..............1⅔
3................85.0	50..............1¾
4............113.4	100............3½

UNITED STATES		UNITED KINGDOM
sl st (slip stitch)	=	sc (single crochet)
sc (single crochet)	=	dc (double crochet)
hdc (half double crochet)	=	htr (half treble crochet)
dc (double crochet)	=	tr (treble crochet)
tr (treble crochet)	=	dtr (double treble crochet)
dtr (double treble crochet)	=	ttr (triple treble crochet)
skip	=	miss

Single crochet decrease (sc dec): (Insert hook, yo, draw lp through) in each of the sts indicated, yo, draw through all lps on hook.

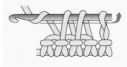

Example of 2-sc dec

Half double crochet decrease (hdc dec): (Yo, insert hook, yo, draw lp through) in each of the sts indicated, yo, draw through all lps on hook.

Example of 2-hdc dec

Reverse single crochet (reverse sc): Ch 1, sk first st, working from left to right, insert hook in next st from front to back, draw up lp on hook, yo and draw through both lps on hook.

Chain (ch): Yo, pull through lp on hook.

Single crochet (sc): Insert hook in st, yo, pull through st, yo, pull through both lps on hook.

Double crochet (dc): Yo, insert hook in st, yo, pull through st, [yo, pull through 2 lps] twice.

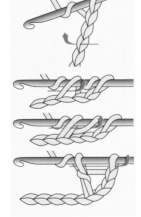

Double crochet decrease (dc dec): (Yo, insert hook, yo, draw lp through, yo, draw through 2 lps on hook) in each of the sts indicated, yo, draw through all lps on hook.

Example of 2-dc dec

Front loop (front lp) Back loop (back lp)

Front Loop   Back Loop

Front post stitch (fp): Back post stitch (bp): When working post st, insert hook from right to left around post of st on previous row.

Back   Front

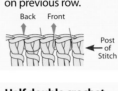

Post of Stitch

Half double crochet (hdc): Yo, insert hook in st, yo, pull through st, yo, pull through all 3 lps on hook.

Double treble crochet (dtr): Yo 3 times, insert hook in st, yo, pull through st, [yo, pull through 2 lps] 4 times.

Treble crochet decrease (tr dec): Holding back last lp of each st, tr in each of the sts indicated, yo, pull through all lps on hook.

Example of 2-tr dec

Slip stitch (sl st): Insert hook in st, pull through both lps on hook.

Chain color change (ch color change) Yo with new color, draw through last lp on hook.

Double crochet color change (dc color change) Drop first color, yo with new color, draw through last 2 lps of st.

Treble crochet (tr): Yo twice, insert hook in st, yo, pull through st, [yo, pull through 2 lps] 3 times.

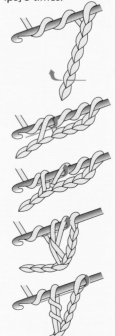

Metric Conversion Charts

METRIC CONVERSIONS

yards	x	.9144	=	metres (m)
yards	x	91.44	=	centimetres (cm)
inches	x	2.54	=	centimetres (cm)
inches	x	25.40	=	millimetres (mm)
inches	x	.0254	=	metres (m)

centimetres	x	.3937	=	inches
metres	x	1.0936	=	yards

INCHES INTO MILLIMETRES & CENTIMETRES (Rounded off slightly)

inches	mm	cm	inches	cm	inches	cm	inches	cm
1/8	3	0.3	5	12.5	21	53.5	38	96.5
1/4	6	0.6	5 1/2	14	22	56	39	99
3/8	10	1	6	15	23	58.5	40	101.5
1/2	13	1.3	7	18	24	61	41	104
5/8	15	1.5	8	20.5	25	63.5	42	106.5
3/4	20	2	9	23	26	66	43	109
7/8	22	2.2	10	25.5	27	68.5	44	112
1	25	2.5	11	28	28	71	45	114.5
1 1/4	32	3.2	12	30.5	29	73.5	46	117
1 1/2	38	3.8	13	33	30	76	47	119.5
1 3/4	45	4.5	14	35.5	31	79	48	122
2	50	5	15	38	32	81.5	49	124.5
2 1/2	65	6.5	16	40.5	33	84	50	127
3	75	7.5	17	43	34	86.5		
3 1/2	90	9	18	46	35	89		
4	100	10	19	48.5	36	91.5		
4 1/2	115	11.5	20	51	37	94		

KNITTING NEEDLES CONVERSION CHART

Canada/U.S.	0	1	2	3	4	5	6	7	8	9	10	10½	11	13	15
Metric (mm)	2	2¼	2¾	3¼	3½	3¾	4	4½	5	5½	6	6½	8	9	10

CROCHET HOOKS CONVERSION CHART

Canada/U.S.	1/B	2/C	3/D	4/E	5/F	6/G	8/H	9/I	10/J	10½/K	N
Metric (mm)	2.25	2.75	3.25	3.5	3.75	4.25	5	5.5	6	6.5	9.0

Annie's® *In a Weekend: Baby Afghans* is published by Annie's, 306 East Parr Road, Berne, IN 46711. Printed in USA. Copyright © 2016 Annie's. All rights reserved. This publication may not be reproduced in part or in whole without written permission from the publisher.

RETAIL STORES: If you would like to carry this publication or any other Annie's publication, visit AnniesWSL.com.

Every effort has been made to ensure that the instructions in this publication are complete and accurate. We cannot, however, take responsibility for human error, typographical mistakes or variations in individual work. Please visit AnniesCustomerService.com to check for pattern updates.

ISBN: 978-1-59012-574-8
1 2 3 4 5 6 7 8 9